Cut and Paste
Alphabet

by Marilynn G. Barr

Publisher: Roberta Suid
Editor: Beverly Cory

Monday Morning is a registered trademark of
Monday Morning Books, Inc.

Entire contents copyright © 1992
by Monday Morning Books, Inc., Box 1680,
Palo Alto, California 94302

For a complete catalog write to the address above.

ISBN 1-878279-34-3

Printed in the United States of America

9 8 7 6

Contents

INTRODUCTION

Cut and Paste Alphabet is a collection of hands-on activities for preschool to first-grade. A monkey, an alligator, and a host of other animals help the children learn to recognize, name, trace, and write the letters of the alphabet. The activities provide practice in following directions and help children develop their fine motor skills through coloring, cutting, pasting, and writing.

All the activities are duplicatable. The children need only crayons, pencils, scissors, and paste. Use the children's completed work for colorful classroom displays, mounting the pages or cut-outs on construction paper or fadeless art paper.

ACTIVITIES

I Can Cut and Paste the Letters (pages 5-17) Cut each page in half if you want to deal with the letters singly or in a different order. If you are also teaching letter sounds, the pictured items (for example, *cat, cup,* and *crown*) can help.

I Can Match Capital and Lowercase (pages 19-23) These pages help the children relate the capital and the lowercase forms of each letter.

I Can Write the Letters (pages 24-37) Children trace and write the letters—capital and lowercase of each—then color and cut out the train cars. To

create the Alphabet Express, make one or two trains of cars posted end-to-end on the classroom wall. Be sure to include samples of each child's work.

Tracing Lines (pages 38-40) Following the arrows and tracing the dots gives practice in making the lines needed for letter formation.

BULLETIN BOARD PATTERN

Monkey Pattern (pages 41-42) Copy, cut, and color the pattern pieces. Use brass fasteners to attach arms and legs, allowing them to move freely. (Mount the arms on the front, and the monkey can play peekaboo.) Pose one or more monkeys on the bulletin board along with children's work. Children can also make their own puppet monkeys from the pattern.

The Alphabet Express See the description of pages 24–37 for a great way to show off children's work and decorate the classroom.

TAKE-HOME ALPHABET BOOK

My Alphabet Book (pages 43-48) This culminating activity provides a review of the letters. Mount the mini-pages on colored paper and staple them together to create take-home keepsakes.

I Can Color, Cut, and Paste B

Directions:
Trace the letters.
Color the picture.
Cut out and paste the letters in place.

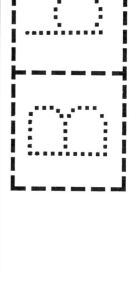

I Can Color, Cut, and Paste A

Directions:
Trace the letters.
Color the picture.
Cut out and paste the letters in place.

Note to Teacher:
Provide each child with a pencil, crayons, scissors, and paste.

5

I Can Color, Cut, and Paste D

Directions:
Trace the letters.
Color the picture.
Cut out and paste the letters in place.

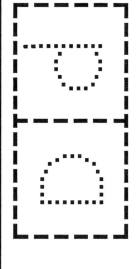

I Can Color, Cut, and Paste C

Directions:
Trace the letters.
Color the picture.
Cut out and paste the letters in place.

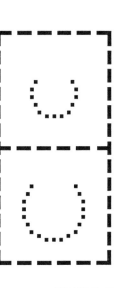

Note to Teacher:
Provide each child with a pencil, crayons, scissors, and paste.

F

I Can Color, Cut, and Paste

Directions:
Trace the letters.
Color the picture.
Cut out and paste the letters in place.

E

I Can Color, Cut, and Paste

Directions:
Trace the letters.
Color the picture.
Cut out and paste the letters in place.

Note to Teacher:
Provide each child with a pencil, crayons, scissors, and paste.

7

I Can Color, Cut, and Paste H

Directions:
Trace the letters.
Color the picture.
Cut out and paste the letters in place.

I Can Color, Cut, and Paste G

Directions:
Trace the letters.
Color the picture.
Cut out and paste the letters in place.

Note to Teacher:
Provide each child with a pencil, crayons, scissors, and paste.

I Can Color, Cut, and Paste J

Directions:
Trace the letters.
Color the picture.
Cut out and paste the letters in place.

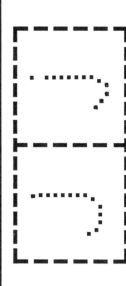

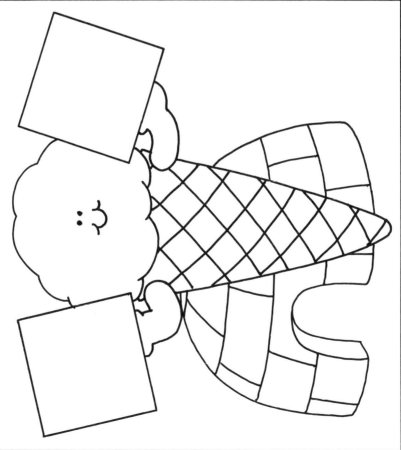

I Can Color, Cut, and Paste I

Directions:
Trace the letters.
Color the picture.
Cut out and paste the letters in place.

Note to Teacher:
Provide each child with a pencil, crayons, scissors, and paste.

I Can Color, Cut, and Paste L

Directions:
Trace the letters.
Color the picture.
Cut out and paste the letters in place.

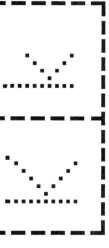

I Can Color, Cut, and Paste K

Directions:
Trace the letters.
Color the picture.
Cut out and paste the letters in place.

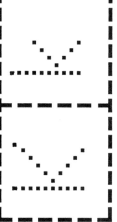

Note to Teacher:
Provide each child with a pencil, crayons, scissors, and paste.

10

I Can Color, Cut, and Paste N

Directions:
Trace the letters.
Color the picture.
Cut out and paste the letters in place.

I Can Color, Cut, and Paste M

Directions:
Trace the letters.
Color the picture.
Cut out and paste the letters in place.

Note to Teacher:
Provide each child with a pencil, crayons, scissors, and paste.

I Can Color, Cut, and Paste P

Directions:
Trace the letters.
Color the picture.
Cut out and paste the letters in place.

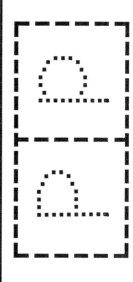

I Can Color, Cut, and Paste O

Directions:
Trace the letters.
Color the picture.
Cut out and paste the letters in place.

Note to Teacher:
Provide each child with a pencil, crayons, scissors, and paste.

I Can Color, Cut, and Paste R

Directions:
Trace the letters.
Color the picture.
Cut out and paste the letters in place.

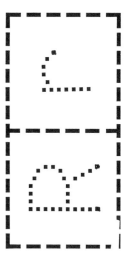

I Can Color, Cut, and Paste Q

Directions:
Trace the letters.
Color the picture.
Cut out and paste the letters in place.

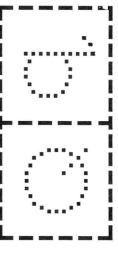

Note to Teacher:
Provide each child with a pencil, crayons, scissors, and paste.

13

I Can Color, Cut, and Paste T

Directions:
Trace the letters.
Color the picture.
Cut out and paste the letters in place.

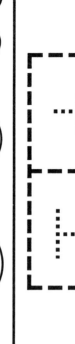

I Can Color, Cut, and Paste S

Directions:
Trace the letters.
Color the picture.
Cut out and paste the letters in place.

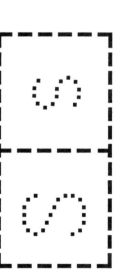

Note to Teacher:
Provide each child with
a pencil, crayons,
scissors, and paste.

14

I Can Color, Cut, and Paste V

Directions:
Trace the letters.
Color the picture.
Cut out and paste the letters in place.

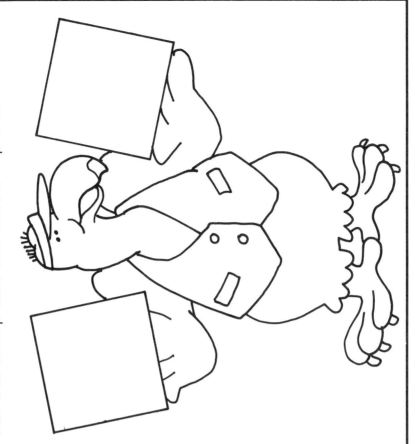

I Can Color, Cut, and Paste U

Directions:
Trace the letters.
Color the picture.
Cut out and paste the letters in place.

Note to Teacher:
Provide each child with a pencil, crayons, scissors, and paste.

I Can Color, Cut, and Paste X

Directions:
Trace the letters.
Color the picture.
Cut out and paste the letters in place.

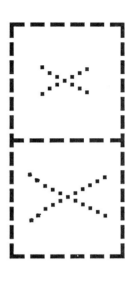

I Can Color, Cut, and Paste W

Directions:
Trace the letters.
Color the picture.
Cut out and paste the letters in place.

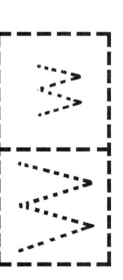

Note to Teacher:
Provide each child with a pencil, crayons, scissors, and paste.

16

I Can Color, Cut, and Paste Z

Directions:
Trace the letters.
Color the picture.
Cut out and paste the letters in place.

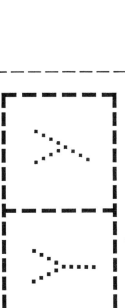

I Can Color, Cut, and Paste Y

Directions:
Trace the letters.
Color the picture.
Cut out and paste the letters in place.

Note to Teacher:
Provide each child with a pencil, crayons, scissors, and paste.

I Can Cut and Paste and Match

Directions:
Color the pictures.
Look at the letter on each sign.
Cut out and paste the matching drums in the correct baskets.

I Can Cut and Paste and Match

Directions:

Color the pictures.

Look at the letter on each bag.

Cut out and paste the cans in the correct bags.

I Can Cut and Paste and Match

Directions:

Color the pictures.

Look at the letter on each tag.

Cut out and paste the matching t-shirts in the correct suitcases.

I Can Cut and Paste and Match

Directions:

Color the pictures.

Look at the letter on each jar.

Cut out and paste the matching pickles in the correct jars.

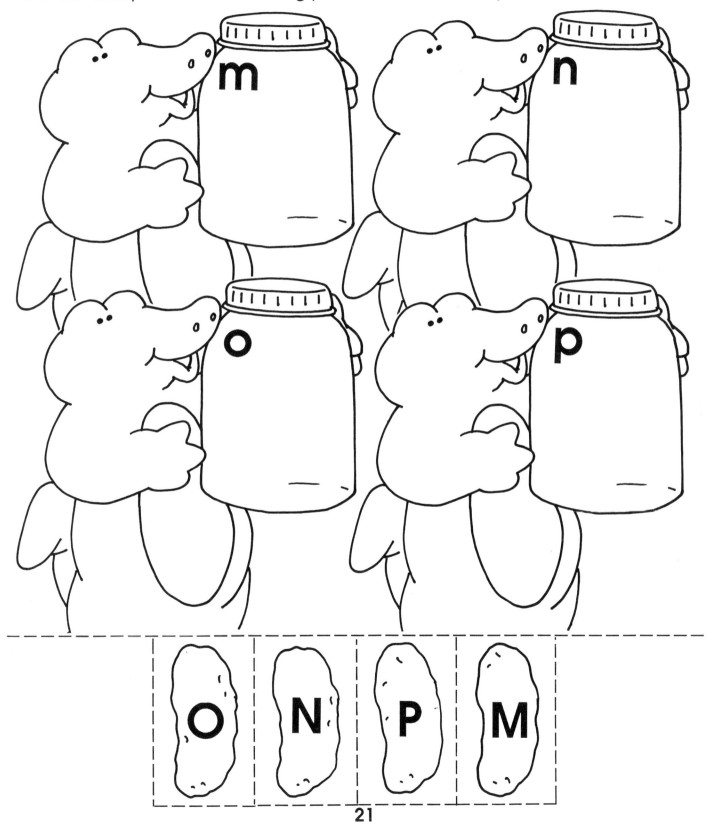

I Can Cut and Paste and Match

Directions:
Color the pictures.
Look at the letter on each pan.
Cut out and paste the matching pancakes in the correct pans.

I Can Cut and Paste and Match

Directions:
Color the pictures.
Look at the letter on each sail.
Cut out and paste the matching sails on the correct boat.

Note to Teacher:
Have children color and cut out the train cars on pages 24-37 for an Alphabet Express display.

Directions:
Color the picture.

The Alphabet Express

Name

A B C D E F G H I J K L M N O P Q R S T U V W X Y Z

24

Directions:
Look at the letters on each line.
Trace the letters.
Then write the letters.

Name _____

I Can Write A and B on the Alphabet Express

A

a

B

b

25

Directions:
Look at the letters on each line.
Trace the letters.
Then write the letters.

Name _____

I Can Write C and D on the Alphabet Express

26

Directions:
Look at the letters on each line.
Trace the letters.
Then write the letters.

Name _____

I Can Write E and F on the Alphabet Express

27

Directions:
Look at the letters on each line.
Trace the letters.
Then write the letters.

Name _____

I Can Write G and H on the Alphabet Express

28

Directions:
Look at the letters on each line.
Trace the letters.
Then write the letters.

Name _____

I Can Write I and J on the Alphabet Express

29

Directions:
Look at the letters on each line.
Trace the letters.
Then write the letters.

Name _____

I Can Write K and L on the Alphabet Express

K

k

L

30

Directions:
Look at the letters on each line.
Trace the letters.
Then write the letters.

Name _____

I Can Write M and N on the Alphabet Express

N N N

n n n

N

n

M M M

m m m m

M

m

31

Directions:
Look at the letters on each line.
Trace the letters.
Then write the letters.

Name _____

I Can Write O and P on the Alphabet Express

32

Directions:
Look at the letters on each line.
Trace the letters.
Then write the letters.

Name

I Can Write Q and R on the Alphabet Express

33

Directions:
Look at the letters on each line.
Trace the letters.
Then write the letters.

Name _____

I Can Write S and T on the Alphabet Express

T   t

S   s

34

Directions:
Look at the letters on each line.
Trace the letters.
Then write the letters.

Name _____

I Can Write U and V on the Alphabet Express

35

Directions:
Look at the letters on each line.
Trace the letters.
Then write the letters.

Name _____

I Can Write W and X on the Alphabet Express

36

Directions:
Look at the letters on each line.
Trace the letters.
Then write the letters.

Name _____

I Can Write Y and Z on the Alphabet Express

I Can Trace from Top to Bottom and Left to Right

Trace the dotted lines.
Follow the arrows.

Name _____

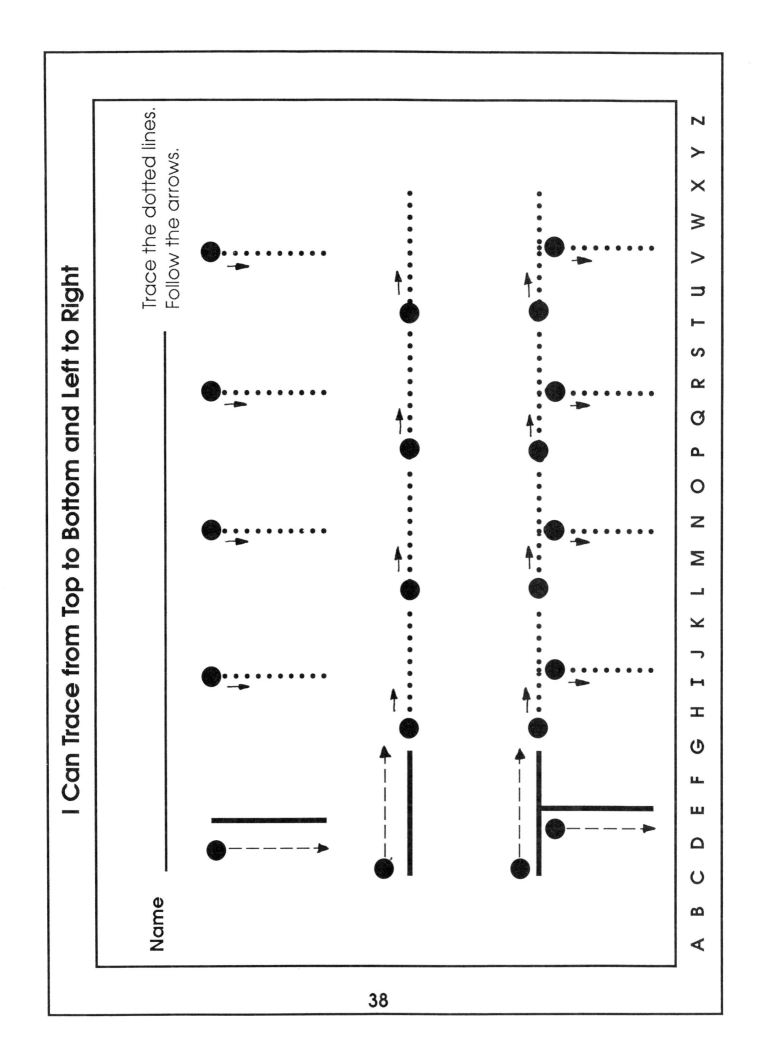

A B C D E F G H I J K L M N O P Q R S T U V W X Y Z

38

I Can Trace a Slant Left and Right and Up and Down

Trace the dotted lines.
Follow the arrows.

Name

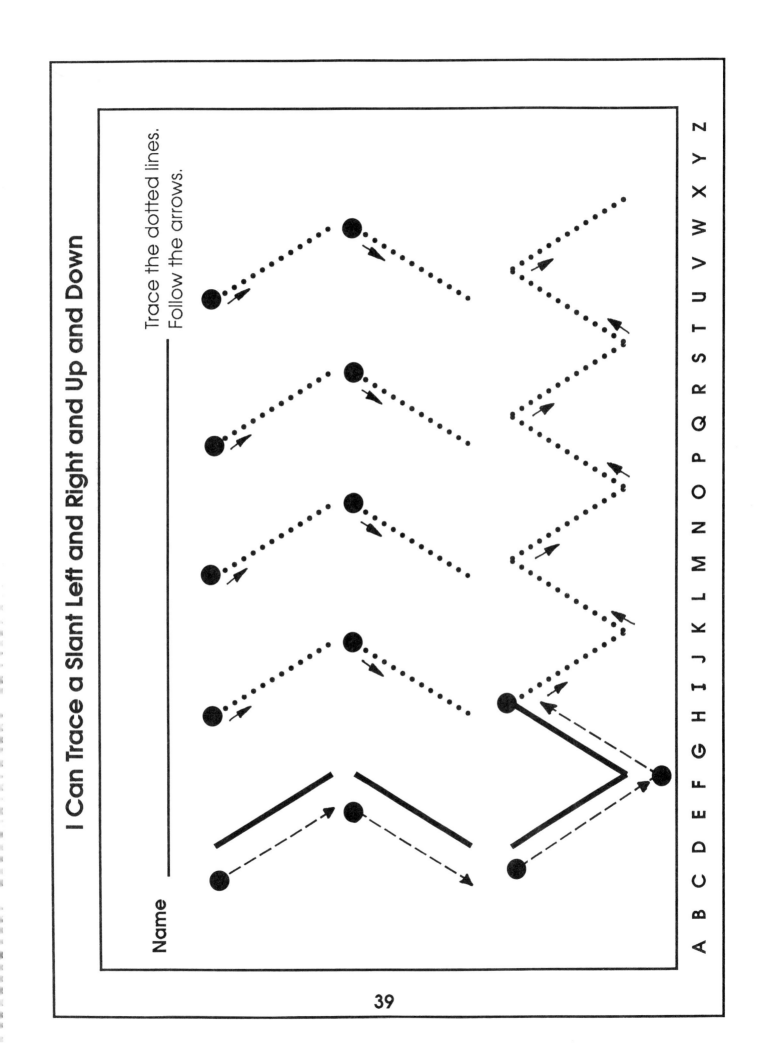

A B C D E F G H I J K L M N O P Q R S T U V W X Y Z

I Can Trace a Curve to the Left and to the Right and Around

Name _____

Trace the dotted lines.
Follow the arrows.

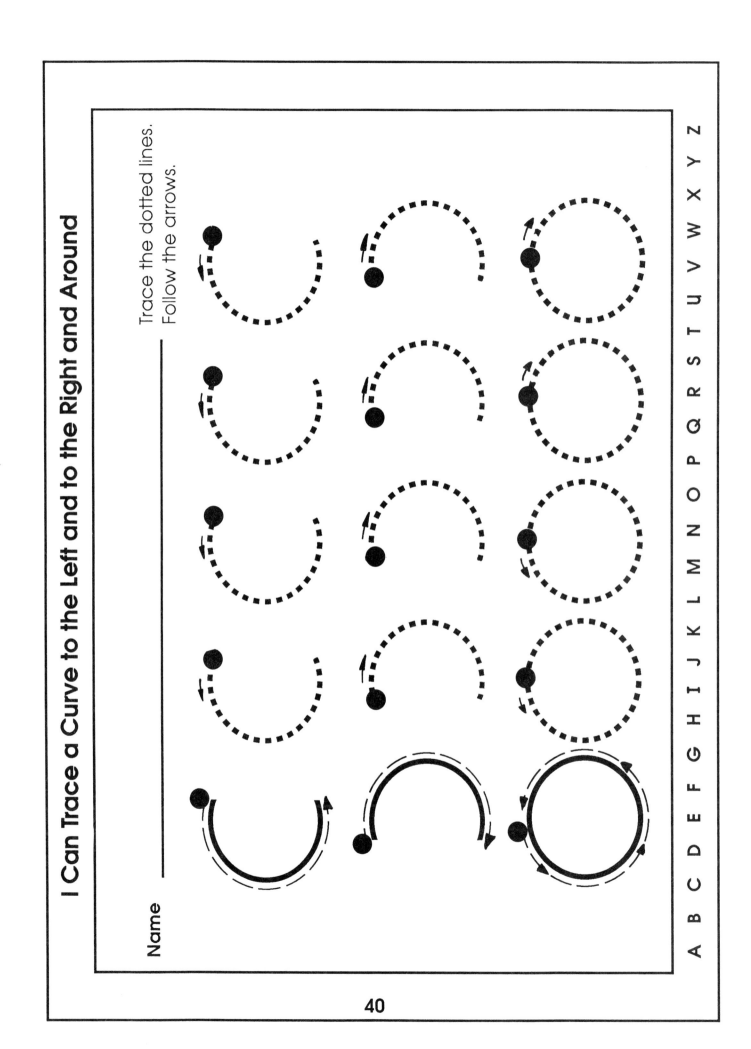

Bulletin Board Pattern

Copy and cut out the monkey pattern on pages 41-42.
Use brass fasteners to attach the movable arms and legs.

Bulletin Board Pattern

Copy and cut out the monkey pattern on pages 41-42.
Use brass fasteners to attach the movable arms and legs.

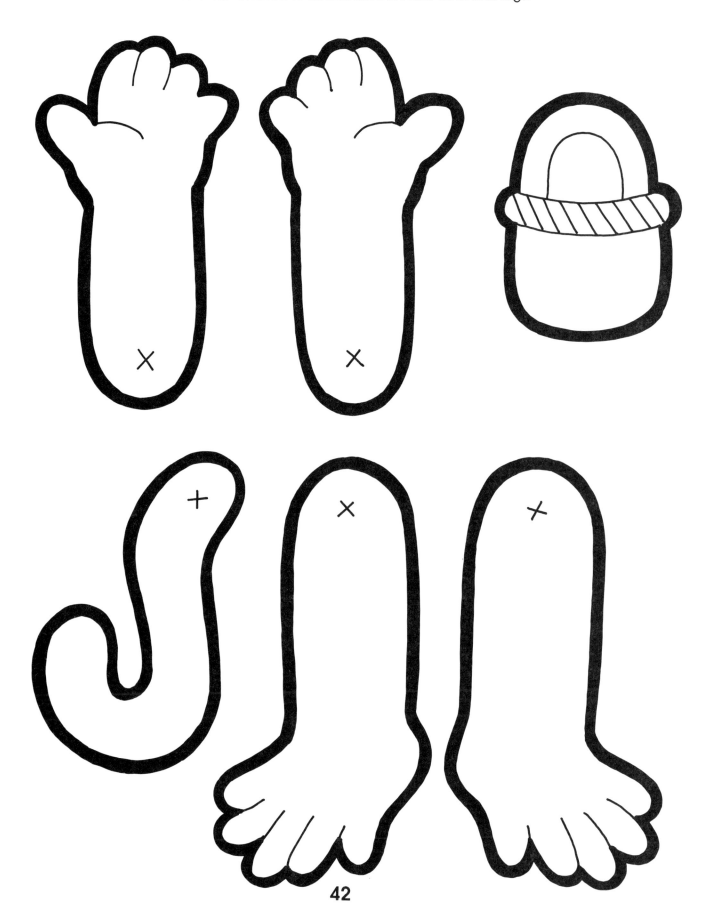

Directions:
Color the picture.
Cut out the page.

Note to Teacher:
Provide each child with crayons, scissors, and paste.
Staple pages 43-48 together to create a take-home
alphabet book.

My
Alphabet
Book

My Alphabet Book

Directions:
Color the letters.
Cut out and paste the letters in place.
Color and cut out the page.

I Can Cut and Paste
the Alphabet

B

D

F

A

C

E

G

My Alphabet Book

Directions:
Color the letters.
Cut out and paste the letters in place.
Color and cut out the page.

I Can Cut and Paste
the Alphabet

VITAMIN D MILK

H   J

L

N   P

I

O

M

K

My Alphabet Book

Directions:
Color the letters.
Cut out and paste the letters in place.
Color and cut out the page.

I Can Cut and Paste
the Alphabet

S

V

Q

R

T   U

My Alphabet Book

Directions:
Color the letters.
Cut out and paste the letters in place.
Color and cut out the page.

I Can Cut and Paste the Alphabet

Y

X

Z

W

My Alphabet Book

Directions:
Write your name on the line.
Color the picture.
Cut out the page.

Student's Name

A, B, C, D, E, F, G,
H, I, J, K,
L, M, N, O, P,
Q, R, S,
T, U, V,
W,
X,
Y, and Z.
Now I know my ABC's.
Next time won't you sing with me.

My Alphabet Book